Jr. Graphic Biographies™

SITTING BULL

and the Battle of the Little Bighorn

Dan Abnett

PowerKiDS press

New York

Published in 2007 by The Rosen Publishing Group, Inc.
29 East 21st Street, New York, NY 10010

First Edition

Editors: Joanne Randolph and Nel Yomtov
Book Design: Julio Gil
Illustrations: Q2A

Library of Congress Cataloging-in-Publication Data

Abnett, Dan.
  Sitting Bull and the Battle of the Little Bighorn / by Dan Abnett.— 1st ed.
      p. cm. — (Jr. graphic biographies)
  Includes index.
  ISBN (10) 1-4042-3394-6 (13) 978-1-4042-3394-2 (lib. bdg.) —
      ' (10) 1-4042-2147-6 (13) 978-1-4042-2147-5 (pbk.)
      ittle Bighorn, Battle of the, Mont., 1876—Juvenile literature. 2. Sitting Bull,
      .?–1890—Juvenile literature. I. Title. II. Series.

  376.A2 2007
  3'2—dc22

                                                              2006001588

      ictured in the United States of America

CONTENTS

MAIN CHARACTERS

Sitting Bull (c. 1831–1890) A Native American **medicine man** and leader of the Lakota Sioux. Sitting Bull often fought against the U.S. Army, which was trying to take lands away from Native Americans. He led thousands of Indian **warriors** against the troops of George Armstrong Custer at the Battle of the Little Bighorn in 1876. Later Sitting Bull took his tribe to Canada in search of freedom from the U.S. government. He returned to the United States in 1881. Government officials feared Sitting Bull's power. When the government sent Indian police to arrest Sitting Bull, he was killed.

George Armstrong Custer (1839–1876) U.S. cavalry commander in the American Civil War and wars against Native Americans. A cavalry is a group of soldiers who ride horses. He is best known for his part in the Battle of the Little Bighorn. He and most of his men were killed in the battle against Native American tribes, led by Sitting Bull.

Crazy Horse (c. 1842–1877) A member of Oglala Sioux Native American tribe. He is remembered for his bravery in battle. Crazy Horse was known among his own people as a great leader. He fought to keep the Lakota way of life and he led his people against white Americans who tried to take Native American lands.

SITTING BULL AND
THE BATTLE OF THE LITTLE BIGHORN

SITTING BULL WAS A LAKOTA SIOUX INDIAN. HE WAS BORN IN SOUTH DAKOTA AROUND 1831.

PEOPLE CALLED HIM "SLOW" BECAUSE HE ALWAYS DID THINGS CAREFULLY AND WELL.

SLOW'S FIRST BATTLE WAS AGAINST A TRIBE CALLED THE CROW. HE WAS 14 YEARS OLD.

SLOW'S FATHER WAS SO PROUD OF HIS SON THAT HE GAVE HIM THE NAME SITTING BULL.

WHEN HE WAS OLDER, SITTING BULL DANCED THE SIOUX SUN DANCE AND BECAME A MEDICINE MAN.

BY THE 1850S, GOLD WAS FOUND ON THE WEST COAST OF AMERICA. MANY PEOPLE PASSED THROUGH SIOUX LANDS IN THE MIDWEST ON THEIR WAY TO FIND GOLD.

THE SIOUX FOUGHT TO KEEP THE WHITE **SETTLERS** FROM TAKING THEIR LAND. HOWEVER, THE U.S. GOVERNMENT OFTEN GAVE SETTLERS LAND THAT BELONGED TO THE NATIVE AMERICANS.

IN A **TREATY** IN 1868, THE GOVERNMENT SET UP **RESERVATIONS** ON WHICH THE NATIVE AMERICANS WERE TO LIVE.

THAT YEAR, SITTING BULL'S UNCLE, CHIEF FOUR HORNS, CALLED A MEETING OF THE SIOUX TRIBES.

HE WANTED TO TALK ABOUT THE **FUTURE** OF HIS PEOPLE.

WE NEED A NEW LEADER TO GUIDE US IN THESE HARD TIMES.

WE SHOULD MAKE SITTING BULL THE LEADER OF ALL THE SIOUX TRIBES.

SITTING BULL WAS MADE THE **SUPREME** CHIEF OF ALL THE SIOUX TRIBES.

SOME NATIVE AMERICANS LIVED ON THE RESERVATIONS. THEY LIVED MORE LIKE WHITE FARMERS THAN LIKE NATIVE AMERICANS.

SITTING BULL AND HIS SIOUX TRIBES KEPT HUNTING AND ENJOYING THE OLD WAY OF LIFE.

THE U.S. GOVERNMENT BUILT ARMY **FORTS** ON SIOUX LANDS.

THE SOLDIERS WERE THERE TO **PROTECT** WHITE SETTLERS FROM NATIVE AMERICANS.

DURING THE 1870S, THE SIOUX ATTACKED THE FORTS SEVERAL TIMES. THERE WERE MANY BATTLES BETWEEN THE SIOUX AND THE ARMY.

MANY SOLDIERS AND SIOUX WARRIORS WERE KILLED AND WOUNDED IN THE BATTLES.

FROM 1870 TO 1872, THE SIOUX FOUGHT AGAINST THE CROW TRIBE. THE SIOUX NEEDED NEW LAND ON WHICH TO LIVE. THEY WON A LOT OF LAND FROM THE CROW.

IN 1872, 2,000 SIOUX WARRIORS GATHERED AT THE YELLOWSTONE RIVER TO ATTACK THE CROW.

THE U.S. ARMY HAD ALSO SET UP CAMP ON THE YELLOWSTONE RIVER.

WE WON THIS LAND FROM THE CROW. WHY IS THE WHITE SETTLER'S ARMY HERE?

GOVERNMENT **ENGINEERS** WERE MEASURING THE LAND. THEY WANTED TO BUILD A RAILROAD. THE ARMY WAS THERE TO PROTECT THEM.

CRAZY HORSE WAS THE CHIEF OF THE OGLALA TRIBE AND A FINE WARRIOR. HE WAS ALSO SITTING BULL'S GOOD FRIEND AND **ADVISER**.

WE FOUGHT HARD FOR THIS LAND. WE CANNOT LIVE WITHOUT IT.

WE WILL DRIVE THE WHITE MEN OUT, CRAZY HORSE.

THE SIOUX ATTACKED, BUT THE U.S. SOLDIERS WERE WELL ARMED.

SITTING BULL WANTED TO SHOW THE SOLDIERS HE DID NOT FEAR THEM. HE PLANNED TO SMOKE HIS PIPE WHERE HE COULD BE HIT BY THEIR **BULLETS**.

FOUR BRAVE SIOUX WARRIORS JOINED SITTING BULL TO SMOKE A PIPE. THE SOLDIERS KEPT FIRING.

IN 1874, GENERAL GEORGE ARMSTRONG CUSTER OF THE U.S. ARMY WAS WORKING IN DAKOTA. ENGINEERS FROM HIS GROUP FOUND GOLD IN THE BLACK HILLS.

THE 1868 TREATY SAID WHITE SETTLERS WERE NOT ALLOWED IN THE BLACK HILLS. THIS WAS THE SIOUX'S LAND. WHITE MEN LOOKING FOR GOLD DECIDED TO GO THERE ANYWAY.

THE GOVERNMENT TRIED TO BUY THE LAND FROM THE SIOUX TRIBES. HOWEVER, SITTING BULL DECIDED NOT TO SELL THE LAND.

THE GOVERNMENT ENDED THE TREATY WITH THE SIOUX. IT **INSISTED** THAT THE SIOUX MUST MOVE TO A RESERVATION BY JANUARY 31, 1876.

THEY WILL NOT TAKE OUR LAND FROM US. THEY WILL NOT MAKE US LIVE ON THEIR RESERVATIONS.

MANY OTHER NATIVE AMERICAN NATIONS WERE AGAINST GIVING UP THEIR LAND, TOO. THE CHEYENNE TRIBE JOINED WITH SITTING BULL'S WARRIORS TO **DEFEND** THE PLAINS.

LONE HORN, CHIEF OF THE MINICONJOU TRIBE, ALSO MET WITH SITTING BULL.

THE BLACK HILLS HAVE FED AND **SHELTERED** THE SIOUX FOR A LONG TIME.

IN THE SPRING OF 1876, THE ARMY BEGAN ATTACKING NATIVE AMERICAN CAMPS.

ALL THE TRIBES MUST WORK TOGETHER. WE MUST DRIVE OUT THE WHITE SOLDIERS.

AT LEAST NINE DIFFERENT NATIVE AMERICAN TRIBES JOINED TO FIGHT THE U.S. ARMY. THEY INCLUDED THE SIOUX, THE CHEYENNE, AND THE MINICONJOU.

MORE THAN 3,500 NATIVE AMERICAN WARRIORS CAMPED IN THE VALLEY OF THE LITTLE BIGHORN RIVER, IN MONTANA.

GENERAL CUSTER GATHERED HIS MEN. HE PLANNED TO SURPRISE THE NATIVE AMERICANS.

THE INDIANS HAVE SEEN US.

WE MUST ATTACK THEM, BEFORE THEY **FLEE** INTO THE COUNTRYSIDE!

ON JUNE 25, GENERAL CUSTER ORDERED MAJOR RENO AND ABOUT 140 MEN TO ATTACK THE NATIVE AMERICAN CAMP AT THE LITTLE BIGHORN.

SITTING BULL HAD A DREAM ABOUT THE COMING BATTLE. HIS DREAM TOLD HIM THAT HIS WARRIORS WOULD WIN.

HUNDREDS OF NATIVE AMERICAN WARRIORS FOUGHT BACK AND KILLED RENO'S MEN.

AFTER BEATING RENO'S MEN, THE NATIVE AMERICAN WARRIORS SAW CUSTER AND HIS MEN ON A NEARBY HILL.

CUSTER'S FORCE OF ABOUT 240 MEN WERE ATTACKED BY BETWEEN 600 TO 1,000 NATIVE AMERICAN WARRIORS. ALL OF CUSTER'S MEN WERE KILLED.

THE BATTLE OF THE LITTLE BIGHORN ALSO BECAME KNOWN AS CUSTER'S LAST STAND.

HOWEVER, SITTING BULL AND HIS PEOPLE STILL FACED HARD TIMES. SOLDIERS BEGAN CHASING AWAY BUFFALO FROM INDIAN HUNTING GROUNDS.

WHITE SETTLERS KILLED ENTIRE BUFFALO HERDS, TOO.

THE ARMY CHASED THE NATIVE AMERICANS INTO CANADA. THE INDIANS LIVED THERE IN **POVERTY** FOR FOUR YEARS.

THERE ARE NO BUFFALO IN CANADA. WE ARE **STARVING**. MANY OF OUR PEOPLE ARE RETURNING TO AMERICA.

ON JULY 19, 1881, THE LAST OF SITTING BULL'S FOLLOWERS TRAVELED DOWN THE MISSOURI RIVER VALLEY. THEY **SURRENDERED** TO THE U.S. ARMY AT FORT BUFORD.

I WISH IT TO BE KNOWN THAT I WAS THE LAST MAN OF MY TRIBE TO SURRENDER MY **RIFLE.**

THE WHITE PEOPLE STILL FEARED SITTING BULL. ON DECEMBER 15, 1890, LAKOTA POLICEMEN CAME TO ARREST SITTING BULL. THEY SHOT AND KILLED HIM.

THE BRAVE SIOUX CHIEF WAS LAID TO REST IN AN UNMARKED GRAVE.

THE END

TIMELINE

1831	Sitting Bull is born in South Dakota.
1845	Sitting Bull fights in his first battle.
1856	Sitting Bull becomes a medicine man and the leader of the Lakota Sioux.
1868	The U.S. government sets up Indian reservations in a treaty with Native Americans.
1870–1872	Battles are fought between the Sioux and Crow tribes.
1872	The Battle of Little Bighorn is fought.
1877	Sitting Bull and his followers move to Canada.
1881	Sitting Bull and his people return to the United States. They surrender to the U.S. government and begin life on a reservation.
1890	Sitting Bull is killed by a group of Indian policemen, sent to take him prisoner.

GLOSSARY

adviser (ed-VY-zur) A person who helps you make decisions.

bullet (BUL-it) An object fired from a gun.

defend (dih-FEND) To guard from harm.

engineers (en-juh-NEERZ) Masters at planning and building engines, machines, roads, and bridges.

flee (FLEE) To run away.

forts (FORTS) Strong buildings or places that can be guarded against an enemy.

future (FYOO-chur) The time that is coming.

insisted (in-SIST-ed) To have said something in a forceful way.

medicine man (MEH-duh-sun MAN) A person who Native Americans believe to be in close touch with the spirit world and to have the power to cure sickness.

poverty (PAH-ver-tee) The state of being poor.

protect (pruh-TEKT) To keep from harm.

reservations (reh-zer-VAY-shunz) Areas of land set aside by the government for Native Americans to live on.

rifle (RY-ful) A kind of large gun.

settlers (SET-lerz) People who move to a new land to live.

sheltered (SHEL-turd) Kept safe.

starving (STARV-ing) Suffering or dying from hunger.

supreme (suh-PREEM) Greatest in power or rank.

surrendered (suh-REN-derd) Gave up.

treaty (TREE-tee) An official agreement, signed and agreed upon by each party.

warriors (WAR-yurz) People who fight in a war.

INDEX

WEB SITES
Due to the changing nature of Internet links, the Rosen Publishing Group, Inc., has developed an online list of Web sites related to the subject of this book. This site is updated regularly. Please use this link to access the list:
www.powerkidslinks.com/jgb/sitbull/